VERY HARD GAL

LOREM · IPSUM

T0005381

Back in ∞.

The Very Hard Book

Idan Ben-Barak   Philip Bunting

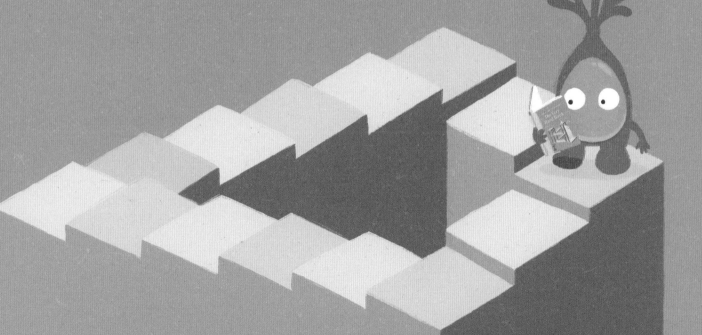

ALLEN&UNWIN
SYDNEY • MELBOURNE • AUCKLAND • LONDON

This book asks you
to do some things.

They are very hard
things to do.

Ready?

Good luck.

Turn this page,
but not yet.

Imagine the
biggest elephant
you can.

Now imagine an even bigger one.

Drop something by accident.

Dig half a hole.

Wag your tail.

Shut your eyes.
Keep them shut.

Now open them.

Forget this line

Sit in an empty room.

Be somewhere else
for a minute.

Make up a joke that makes you laugh.

Make up a new colour.

Do something you don't want to do.

Forge
line, t

t this

oo

What colour is this?

Red.

Let's try again: what colour is this word?

Green.

One more time: what colour is this word written in?

Blue.

Stop thinking about purple turtles.

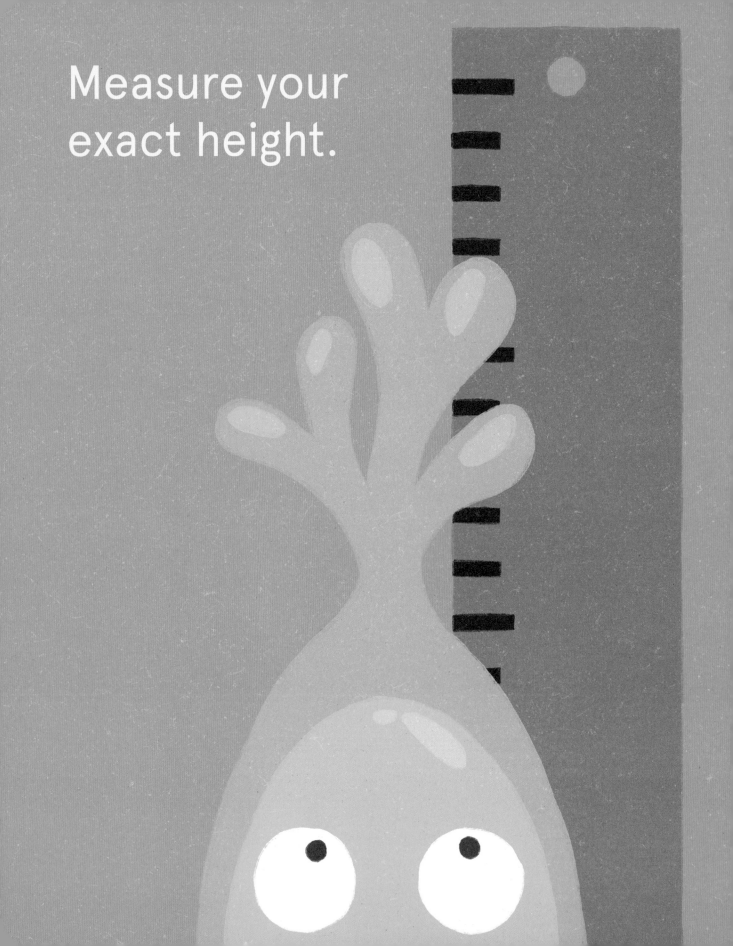

Stop your hair from growing for an hour.

Stop thinking for a minute.

Wake up
now.

Read this book for
the first time again.

Idan Ben-Barak drinks tea,
wears hats, writes books for children,
and thinks he might be wrong.

Philip Bunting's children say
his brain is the size of a pea.
He thinks they might be right.

First published by Allen & Unwin in 2022

Allen & Unwin
83 Alexander Street
Crows Nest NSW 2065
Australia
Phone: (61 2) 8425 0100
Email: info@allenandunwin.com
Web: www.allenandunwin.com

A catalogue record for this
work is available from the
National Library of Australia

NATIONAL
LIBRARY
OF AUSTRALIA

ISBN (AUS hb) 978 1 76052 622 1
ISBN (UK pb) 978 1 91167 954 7
ISBN (AUS pb) 978 1 76106 844 7

For teaching resources, explore allenandunwin.com/resources/for-teachers

Cover and text design by Philip Bunting
Set in Plantin Headline and Apercu

This book was printed in April 2022
by C&C Offset, China

1 3 5 7 9 10 8 6 4 2

MIX
Paper from
responsible sources
FSC® C008047
FSC
www.fsc.org

The Very Hard Gallery

1. Language can play tricks. If you were a computer you'd be stuck, but your mind knows to ignore rules sometimes.
2. Our mind isn't very good at thinking about infinity. But it's fun to try.
3. Some things we intend to do. Other things we do by accident. Can one thing be both?
4. The Heap Problem: When does a thing start being itself?
5. It's absurd. Although… we used to have them, you know.
6. Shhh…
7. The Liar's Paradox: A sentence that contradicts itself. Very confusing.
8. Impossible, because that's not what the word 'empty' means.
9. Wherever you go, you're always here.
10. Surprise is the essence of humour – but can you surprise yourself?
11. Is this about colours or about their names?
12. Failure to Refer: Do things have to be real for us to know them?
13. Free will: If you didn't want to, why did you do it?